# WORLD WAR I
## THROUGH THE EYES OF
# WOODROW WILSON

by Amanda Lanser

**Content Consultant**
Alison Steigerwald, MA
World War I History
University of North Carolina at Charlotte

**Core Library**

An Imprint of Abdo Publishing
abdopublishing.com

abdopublishing.com

Published by Abdo Publishing, a division of ABDO, PO Box 398166, Minneapolis, Minnesota 55439. Copyright © 2016 by Abdo Consulting Group, Inc. International copyrights reserved in all countries. No part of this book may be reproduced in any form without written permission from the publisher. Core Library™ is a trademark and logo of Abdo Publishing.

Printed in the United States of America, North Mankato, Minnesota
082015
012016

THIS BOOK CONTAINS
RECYCLED MATERIALS

Cover Photo: Bettmann/Corbis/AP Images
Interior Photos: Bettmann/Corbis/AP Images, 1; World History Archive/Newscom, 4; Library of Congress, 6; PA Wire/AP Images, 8; AP Images, 10, 30, 32; DPA/Picture-Alliance/DPA/AP Images, 14; Picture History/Newscom, 16; Everett Collection/Newscom, 22, 26; Corbis, 24, 37, 45; Shutterstock Images, 28 (background); Mondadori/Newscom, 34; Bettmann/Corbis, 38

Editor: Jon Westmark
Series Designer: Laura Polzin

**Library of Congress Control Number: 2015945413**

**Cataloging-in-Publication Data**
Lanser, Amanda.
 World War I through the eyes of Woodrow Wilson / Amanda Lanser.
   p. cm. -- (Presidential perspectives)
ISBN 978-1-68078-035-2 (lib. bdg.)
Includes bibliographical references and index.
1. World War, 1914-1918--United States--Juvenile literature.  2. Wilson, Woodrow, 1856-1924--Juvenile literature.   3. Presidents--United States--Juvenile literature.
I. Title.
940.4--dc23
                                                              2015945413

# CONTENTS

**CHAPTER ONE**
**The Weight of War** . . . . . . . . . . **4**

**CHAPTER TWO**
**Navigating Neutrality** . . . . . . . .**14**

**CHAPTER THREE**
**Finishing the Fight** . . . . . . . . **22**

**CHAPTER FOUR**
**Ending the War Fairly** . . . . . . **30**

Important Dates . . . . . . . . . . . . . . . . . . . . . . . . .42

Stop and Think . . . . . . . . . . . . . . . . . . . . . . . . .44

Glossary . . . . . . . . . . . . . . . . . . . . . . . . . . . . . 46

Learn More . . . . . . . . . . . . . . . . . . . . . . . . . . . .47

Index . . . . . . . . . . . . . . . . . . . . . . . . . . . . . . . .48

About the Author . . . . . . . . . . . . . . . . . . . . . . . .48

# CHAPTER ONE

# THE WEIGHT OF WAR

Echoes of applause rang in President Woodrow Wilson's ears as he sat in the White House. It was the evening of April 2, 1917. Less than an hour before, he had delivered a speech. All the members of Congress and the Supreme Court were at the gathering. The speech gave reasons why the United States should enter World War I (1914–1918).

Woodrow Wilson decided after nearly three years the United States could no longer stay out of World War I.

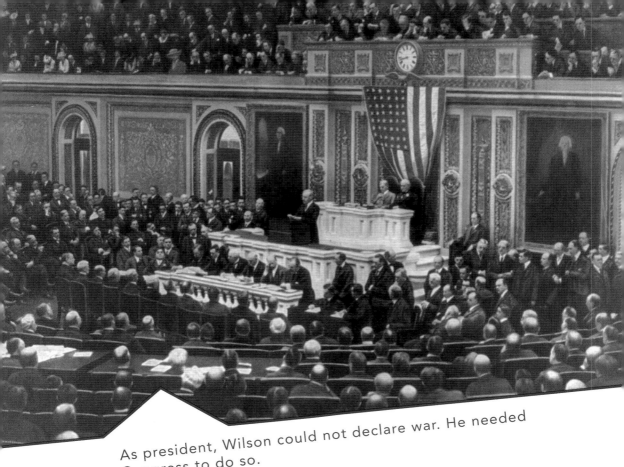

As president, Wilson could not declare war. He needed Congress to do so.

Wilson's speech brought the crowd to its feet. But after he left the podium, Wilson fell silent. His silence lasted through his car ride to the White House. Wilson finally spoke to his private secretary, Joseph Tumulty. "Think about what it was they were applauding," he said. "My message today was a message of death for our young men. How strange it seems to applaud that." A few minutes later, Wilson laid his head down on the table and wept.

World War I had been raging for nearly three years. Since the war began on July 28, 1914, Wilson had promised to keep the United States neutral. But after his speech, he made a confession to Tumulty. Wilson told Tumulty he had known the United States could not stay out of the conflict forever. It took Congress just four days to discuss and vote. On April 6, 1917, the Senate and House of Representatives voted to declare war against Germany.

## U-boats and the *Lusitania*

Wilson's request for war was prompted by German military action. Since fighting started in 1914, Germany used submarines called U-boats against British ships. But the U-boats did not only attack military ships. They also went after trade ships.

On May 1, 1915, the British ship *Lusitania* left New York for the United Kingdom. A week into the

The *Lusitania* was attacked as it passed south of Ireland.

trip, a German U-boat hit the *Lusitania* with a torpedo. The boat sank in just 18 minutes. Nearly 2,000 people were killed, including more than 120 Americans.

On May 11, Wilson wrote to the German government. He said trade ships had the right to travel without being attacked. Germany replied one month later. The government was saddened by the loss of US lives. But it claimed the *Lusitania* had been carrying ammunition and weapons.

Wilson sent another note to the German government. He challenged its claim that there were weapons aboard the *Lusitania*. The Germans said they would not stop submarine warfare. But they would protect US ships as long as no weapons were aboard.

### The *Lusitania*

People in the United States and United Kingdom were outraged by the attack on the *Lusitania*. Since the ship was carrying passengers, it seemed that Germany was attacking defenseless people. But the *Lusitania* had more on board than people. It was also carrying ammunition for rifles and other weapons. Germany had warned the *Lusitania* before it was sunk. The country felt right in sinking the ship.

German U-boats often travelled on the surface before going underwater to attack.

With few exceptions, Germany kept its promise for more than a year and a half. In March 1916, a U-boat sunk a French passenger ship, the *Sussex*. Two Americans were hurt. The United States once again warned Germany. The German government promised to warn passenger and trade ships of enemy countries before it attacked. But on February 1, 1917, German submarines began sinking trade ships.

## The Zimmermann Telegram

The sinking of the *Lusitania* and other trade ships was not the only reason Wilson asked for war. In January 1917, British officials decoded a telegram from Germany to Mexico. German Foreign Minister Arthur Zimmermann asked Mexico to join Germany in the war. In exchange, Germany promised to give Mexico land that the

United States had taken after the Mexican–American War (1846–1848).

After Wilson learned of the message, he went before Congress. He asked it to approve money for weapons to defend US ships. The House of Representatives passed a bill. But the Senate did not.

Wilson was saddened by the response from Congress. But then the public took action. On March 1, US newspapers published the German telegram. It caused outrage. Americans began to favor the war against Germany.

## Wilson's Address to Congress

On Tuesday, March 20, Wilson met with his cabinet. Some of them had pushed for war since 1914. Others had advised Wilson not to enter the fight. But on March 20, all agreed war was the only option. Wilson took a few days to think over the big decision.

On Monday, April 2, Wilson entered the US Capitol. The members of the Senate, the House of Representatives, and the Supreme Court were all there. So were representatives from other countries, including Mexico. Wilson's fingers trembled. The room was quiet as Wilson began to speak.

The president described Germany's actions over the previous three years. He talked about U-boat attacks, violations of international law, and Germany's disregard for human life. Wilson said the United States had a duty to make the world safe for democracy. Congress agreed. It declared war against Germany on April 6, 1917.

## FURTHER EVIDENCE

What was the main idea of Chapter One? Use evidence from the text to support your answer. Then go to the website below. How does the source support the chapter's main idea? List at least two new facts from the website.

### US Entry into World War I
mycorelibrary.com/woodrow-wilson

# NAVIGATING NEUTRALITY

**W**orld War I began on July 28, 1914. A Serbian assassin had killed the future leader of Austria-Hungary, Franz Ferdinand. In response Austria-Hungary declared war on Serbia. Over the next few days, Russia declared war on Serbia. Germany declared war on Russia, France, and Belgium. And the United Kingdom declared war on Germany. Wilson had to figure out how to respond.

Austro-Hungarian and German troops march through Warsaw in 1915.

As president, Wilson made tough decisions about how involved the United States should be in World War I.

## Staying Out of It

On August 19, Wilson issued a proclamation of neutrality. The announcement made it illegal for Americans to join the militaries of warring nations. It created rules that allowed warring nations to continue to use US ports and waters.

Two weeks later, Wilson addressed Congress. He wanted to explain why he was keeping the United States out of the war. He said that Americans came from many different countries. Many had family from Germany. Some supported Germany's actions in the war. Other Americans were of Irish descent. Many of these people did not want the United States to side with the British, because they had mistreated the Irish.

## An Economic Tightrope

The US economy had been doing poorly for nearly two years when World War I started in 1914. Things got worse during the war. European countries converted their trade ships to military ones. There were no ships to bring American goods to Europe.

At the same time, European countries were blocking one another's trade routes. The United Kingdom attacked ships headed to Germany. Germany responded with its own attacks. Few US goods were getting through to feed and supply people across Europe.

In 1914, France approached the US bank J. P. Morgan. The country wanted a loan to help pay for its war costs. But J. P. Morgan was worried that making the loan was illegal. The bank asked for Wilson's guidance. At first Wilson was against the loan. He

## He Kept Us Out of War

While Wilson worked to keep the United States out of the war, he also had to run for reelection. Many Republicans thought Wilson should not have kept the United States neutral. But many other US citizens supported Wilson's approach. His vice president, Thomas Marshall, explained why. "War was [disgusting] to the great mass of Americans," he said. Wilson won reelection in 1916. Marshall said Wilson's success was largely due to his ability to keep the United States out of the war.

thought it would lead to loans with other countries. It would look like the United States was taking sides. It could divide Americans.

But Wilson soon changed his mind. He allowed US companies to sell credits. Warring nations could use the credits to buy US goods. Wilson made it clear that all nations could apply for these credits. He thought this would allow the United States to stay neutral. But by 1917, the United Kingdom and France had received ten times more credits than Germany.

## Unrestricted Submarine Warfare

Since the start of the war, German U-boats had been attacking British trade ships. At first they allowed the passengers and crew aboard these ships to escape. But this required the subs to surface. The United Kingdom started disguising warships as trade ships. When the U-boats surfaced, the warships sunk them.

Germany changed its methods in February 1915. U-boats began sinking British trade ships without warning. Germany called its new tactic "unrestricted submarine warfare." The *Lusitania* was sunk under this tactic.

Wilson's May 11 letter stopped unrestricted submarine warfare temporarily. But Wilson remained cautious. In December 1915, he called on Congress to increase the size of the armed forces. He claimed it must be done to maintain peace.

On February 1, 1917, Germany restarted unrestricted submarine warfare. Wilson once again addressed Congress. He suggested a tactic he called

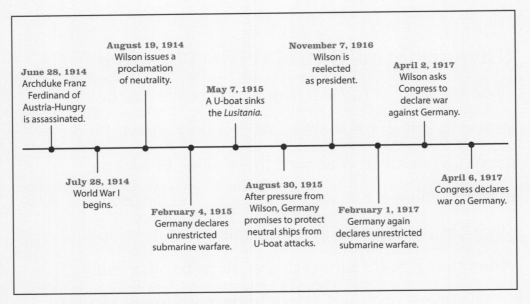

**From Neutrality to War**
A lot occurred before the United States joined World War I.
How does seeing the information laid out together help
you understand the events leading up to the United States
declaring war on Germany?

"armed neutrality." He asked Congress for money to
make weapons to defend US trade ships.

Several senators believed arming US trade ships
brought the country too close to war. They delayed a
vote on the plan until a new Congress took over.

Wilson's plan never passed. But the nation had
drawn closer to war. In just one month, Wilson would
ask Congress to declare war on Germany.

On December 8, 1914, Wilson delivered his second annual address to Congress:

*We are at peace with all the world. . . . From the first we have had a clear and settled policy with regard to military establishments. We never have had, and while we retain our present principles and ideals we never shall have, a large standing army. . . . We shall not alter our attitude toward it because some amongst us are nervous and excited. . . . We have not been negligent of national defense. We are not unmindful of the great responsibility resting upon us. . . . [W]e strive to show in our life as a nation what liberty . . . may do for men and for societies, for individuals, for states, and for mankind.*

Source: Gerhard Peters and John T. Woolley. "Woodrow Wilson: Second Annual Message, December 8, 1914." The American Presidency Project. University of California, Santa Barbara, 2015. Web. Accessed March 20, 2015.

## Changing Minds

This section of Wilson's speech discusses whether the United States should expand its military. Wilson believed the United States did not need to do so. Imagine your friend disagrees with Wilson. Write a short essay to try to change your friend's mind. Back up your opinion with facts and details that support your reasons.

# FINISHING THE FIGHT

Before Wilson's speech to Congress, the United States had declared war on another country only four times. It took four days for Congress to decide to go to war again. On April 6, Wilson announced that the United States was at war with Germany. Declaring war was simple. Getting the country ready to send troops to Europe was not. Wilson got started right away.

Many US women worked in factories to help the war effort.

US Secretary of War Newton Baker pulls out the first number of the draft lottery.

## Strengthening the Military

Wilson asked Congress to strengthen the country's existing military. Only 300,000 men served in the military when the United States declared war. Wilson directed the US Navy to put all its ships into active service. The navy also seized 91 German ships that were in US ports. The crews were sent back to Germany.

Wilson signed a national draft into law. The Selective Service Act went into effect on May 18. Over

18 months, 25 million men were registered for the draft. By the end of the war, 4.4 million men served.

Wilson created government agencies to manage the country's wartime efforts. These groups helped government departments and private businesses work together. The Council of National Defense included members of Wilson's cabinet and business leaders. It managed how supplies got to US troops in Europe.

## Helping the Home Front

Wilson also created agencies to help the US economy during the war. These groups helped manage trade, industry, and raising money for the war effort. They included the War Trade Board, the War Savings Stamps Campaign, and the National War Labor Board.

Wilson asked US businesses to produce quick services, such as faster shipping, to help the war effort. He said businesses should sacrifice big profits for the good of the country. He urged housewives to sacrifice too. Women were told to cut down on the waste their families produced. The government

A banner during a Liberty Loan campaign encourages Americans to save food.

promoted "Meatless Mondays" and "Wheatless Wednesdays." These days were meant to save more food for the troops.

Wilson established daylight saving time. It gave farmers more daylight to work in their fields. In some communities, high school boys were allowed to leave school to help at home. They earned their diplomas by working on the family farm.

Wilson hoped asking Americans to give money would get them to support the war. He started Liberty Loan drives, asking citizens to buy war bonds. The bonds would help pay for supplies for troops. The plan worked. The first Liberty Loan drive raised $1 billion in one month. Four drives raised a total of $17 billion.

## Commander-in-Chief

Wilson was not an experienced military man. As commander-in-chief, he led mainly through his words. He addressed the sailors on the *Pennsylvania* before they headed across the Atlantic Ocean. He urged them to be brave and daring, saying, "That is exactly the thing that the other side does not understand."

## PERSPECTIVES

### Disagreement at Home

Not all Americans were happy about entering World War I. Many German Americans disagreed with Wilson's decision to go to war. Socialists and pacifists were also against it. Socialists favor public control over decisions made by the government. They called the war a crime against Americans. They thought the draft went against the idea that US citizens were free. Pacifists oppose all war. Pacifists called for peace and an end to World War I. Many were thought of as unpatriotic because of this.

1. Honest, public diplomacy
2. Absolute freedom of the seas
3. Fair trade agreements between nations
4. Militaries for national defense only
5. Input from native peoples living in colonial territories
6. Foreign troops leave Russia, and the world treats the country with goodwill
7. Foreign troops leave Belgium, and the country's borders are restored
8. Foreign troops leave France; the country's borders are restored
9. Italy regains territory along its northern border
10. Austro-Hungarians allowed to rule themselves
11. Foreign troops leave Serbia, Romania, and Montenegro, and all borders are restored
12. Turkey is allowed to rule itself outside of the Ottoman Empire
13. Poland becomes a country
14. A general association of nations is formed

**Wilson's 14 Points**
Wilson presented his 14 points for peace to Congress in January 1918. How many of the points specifically address World War I? Do you think these points are more significant than the more general points about world peace? Why or why not?

American troops were winning battles by the end of May 1918. One of their largest successes was the Battle of Belleau Wood. The month-long battle was part of the last German offensive. The war would be over within five months.

## Plan for Peace

While US troops fought in Europe, Wilson planned for peace. On January 8, 1918, he presented his ideas in a speech. It became known as Wilson's 14 Points. He declared that ships must be able to travel freely. National armies must be reduced. And countries should get back lands they lost in the war.

Wilson's final point called for an association of nations, which would preserve member nations' independence and lands. It would become known as the League of Nations.

## EXPLORE ONLINE

Wilson's 14 Points speech became the basis of the peace agreement that ended World War I. Read the information on the 14 points at the website below. How does this information compare to what is in the text? How is it different?

14 Points
mycorelibrary.com/woodrow-wilson

# ENDING THE WAR FAIRLY

By October 1918, Germany was running low on supplies, troops, and morale. It asked for an end to the fighting. Germany hoped Wilson's 14 points would be the terms of the agreement. His terms were not as harsh as the terms of the French and British.

The armistice was signed on November 11, 1918. It required fighting to stop within six hours of its

People in New York City celebrate the armistice with a parade and confetti.

Wilson, *right*, meets with leaders from France, the United Kingdom, and Italy.

signing. Germany was subject to more than a dozen demands. Its troops had to withdraw immediately. It had to give up 5,000 artillery guns, 25,000 machine guns, and 1,700 airplanes. It also gave up 160 U-boats, 5,000 locomotives, and land in East Africa.

Wilson announced the agreement to Congress the same day. He entered the chamber to a standing ovation. He told the crowd, "This tragical war, whose consuming flames swept from one nation to another until all the world was on fire, is at an end." Wilson explained the terms of the armistice. He declared that it was a turning point in the history of the world.

## The Paris Peace Conference

Wilson traveled to Paris, France, two months after the signing of the armistice. He met with representatives from other countries involved in the war. The group was tasked with creating a peace treaty to officially end World War I.

Some people in the United States thought Wilson should have sent someone else to the Paris Peace Conference. They said Wilson's presence at the conference took away his power. No US president had ever gone to such a conference before. But Wilson insisted on going. He was confident in his ability to speak with the representatives at the conference.

## Arguing for the League of Nations

From the start of the Paris Peace Conference on January 12, 1919, Wilson had one goal. He hoped to incorporate the League of Nations into the peace

Wilson, center, leads a parade honoring veterans on February 27, 1919, after his return from the Paris Peace Conference.

treaty. But drafting the treaty would take more than a month. The nations could not agree on the terms. Wilson wanted the treaty to focus on the future, not Germany's past wrongs. But the United Kingdom and France had suffered greatly in the war. They wanted Germany to be punished.

Despite these differences, Wilson drafted a charter for the League of Nations. He presented it to the conference on February 14. There were 26 articles in the charter. Wilson believed the tenth was the most important. It said that if a nation in the league were attacked, the other nations must come to its aid. Wilson believed this was the only way to secure peace.

Wilson returned to the United States shortly after his presentation. The conference was not over. But Wilson had been away longer than any other president had before. He had to build support for the League of Nations at home. One of his biggest opponents was Senator Henry Cabot Lodge. Lodge did not believe a group of nations should have a say in how the United States governed itself.

Wilson expected Lodge's hostility. Before leaving his ship, Wilson spoke out against the opposition. He said that not joining the League of Nations would doom the country to isolation. Lodge fired back. He warned that the final treaty had to maintain US ideals. It could not require the country to enter a foreign war.

It also could not allow other nations to interfere with issues on US soil.

Wilson returned to Paris to find the treaty greatly altered. The United Kingdom and France had changed the terms. The treaty now included severer punishments for Germany.

## The Treaty of Versailles

The final treaty was presented to Germany on May 7, 1919. The terms mirrored those of the armistice. It also included some ideas from Wilson's 14 points. It limited the size of Germany's army. Germany was forced to give up territories in Belgium, Poland, and Czechoslovakia. Article 231 of the treaty was called the "War Guilt Clause." Germany was

### A War to End All Wars

By the end of World War I, 65 million men had been sent to fight. This included 4.4 million US troops. The death toll of the war was more than 8.5 million, including more than 116,500 US servicemen. It had been the bloodiest conflict in the history of Europe.

Wilson leads a parade through Versailles, France, following the signing of the Treaty of Versailles.

required to take full responsibility for World War I. The document also included the charter for the League of Nations. Any nation that approved the treaty would become a member. Germany, the United Kingdom, France, and Italy signed it on June 28, 1919.

Wilson presented the treaty to the US Congress on July 10. Congress would have to approve the terms for the United States to join the League of

Wilson speaks to the public in Tacoma, Washington, on September 18, 1919, to raise support for the League of Nations.

Nations. Wilson still had to win over some members in Congress, including opponents like Lodge.

The president toured to build support for the treaty. His schedule was intense. Many around him feared for his health. In Pueblo, Colorado, Wilson looked very tired. For the first time, he had to restart lines in his speech. He made unexpected pauses. Despite these setbacks, Wilson believed so strongly in his cause he was moved to tears during his speech.

## A Major Setback

Wilson's health took a turn for the worse after the speech in Colorado. He had a stroke later that night. In the next few days, he would have another one. It made it impossible for him to speak in public. Wilson returned to Washington, DC. He continued to serve as president. But he could not do the work necessary to win support for the treaty. On March 15, 1920, the Senate voted on the treaty. It was rejected by a margin of only seven votes.

Wilson turned solemn when he learned of the vote. He regretted he had not been able to stay healthy long enough to gain more support for the treaty. The United States never accepted the Treaty of Versailles or became part of the League of Nations.

## Germany's Raw Deal

The Treaty of Versailles included tough punishments for Germany. The German government called the treaty a diktat, or "dictated peace." Most Germans felt the agreement was unfair. Soon political groups formed. One in particular promised to strengthen Germany's military, regain its land, and rebuild its power in Europe. The group was called the Nazi Party. The Nazi Party and its leader, Adolf Hitler, controlled the German government in the 1930s. The party's actions led to World War II (1939–1945).

Instead it formed separate treaties with Germany and its allies.

Without the United States, the League of Nations was less effective than Wilson had hoped. Germany began pushing back against the harsh terms of the Treaty of Versailles. The US did not get involved because it had not signed the treaty. By the late 1930s, war in Europe once again loomed.

The following passage is the opening from the Covenant of the League of Nations:

*The high contracting parties, in order to promote international co-operation and to achieve international peace and security, by the acceptance of obligations not to resort to war, by the prescription of open, just and honorable relations between nations, by the firm establishment of the understandings of international law as the actual rule of conduct among Governments, and by the maintenance of justice and a scrupulous respect for all treaty obligations in the dealings of organised peoples with one another, agree to this Covenant of the League of Nations.*

Source: "Treaty of Versailles, 1919." Holocaust Encyclopedia. United States Holocaust Memorial Museum, June 20, 2014. Web. Accessed April 10, 2015.

## Consider Your Audience

This passage was written for world leaders. Review the passage carefully. Think about how you would change it for a different audience, such as your siblings, classmates, or parents. Write a new opening for the covenant that includes the same information. But write it so your new audience can understand it.

# IMPORTANT DATES

**July 28, 1914**

Austria-Hungary declares war on Serbia, starting World War I.

**Aug. 4, 1914**

Woodrow Wilson announces the United States will remain neutral in World War I.

**May 7, 1915**

German U-boats sink the *Lusitania*.

**April 2, 1917**

Wilson asks Congress to declare war against Germany.

**April 6, 1917**

Congress declares war against Germany.

**May 18, 1917**

The Selective Service Act goes into effect, starting a national draft.

**Nov. 7, 1916**

Wilson is reelected as president.

**Jan. 1917**

The British decode the Zimmermann Telegram.

**Feb. 1, 1917**

Germany resumes unrestricted submarine warfare.

**Jan. 8, 1918**

Wilson delivers his 14 Points speech.

**Nov. 11, 1918**

World War I ends at the eleventh hour of the eleventh day of the eleventh month.

**June 28, 1919**

The Treaty of Versailles is signed, officially ending the war. Congress blocks the United States from signing.

# STOP AND THINK

## Say What?

Reading about a US president and world history can mean learning a lot of new vocabulary. Find five words in this book you've never heard before. Use a dictionary to find out what they mean. Then write the meanings in your own words, and use each word in a new sentence.

## Take a Stand

In 1914 many US citizens were German immigrants or had German ancestors. Some did not support the United States entering the war. Put yourself in their shoes. Would you want President Wilson to go to war with Germany? Or would you want the United States to remain neutral? Use evidence from Chapter Two to support your opinion.

## Tell the Tale

Chapter Four describes the trip Wilson took to promote the Treaty of Versailles. Imagine you are making a similar trip. Write 200 words about how you would convince the American people to support the treaty. Use evidence from this book to help make your points.

## Dig Deeper

After reading this book, what questions do you still have about Woodrow Wilson? With an adult's help, find a few reliable sources that can help you answer your questions. Write a paragraph about what you learned.

# GLOSSARY

**agencies**
parts of a government that manage specific areas

**armistice**
an agreement to stop fighting

**assassin**
a person who murders an important political person

**cabinet**
a group of advisers to the president

**charter**
an official document

**draft**
selecting people to serve in the military

**neutrality**
a policy of not taking sides in a war

**proclamation**
a formal, public announcement

**tactic**
a planned action or strategy

**telegram**
a message sent by code through wires

# LEARN MORE

## Books

Frith, Margaret. *Who Was Woodrow Wilson?* New York: Grosset & Dunlap, 2015.

Kenney, Karen Latchana. *Everything World War I.* Washington, DC: National Geographic Children's Books, 2014.

Rasmussen, R. Kent. *World War I for Kids: A History with 21 Activities.* Chicago: Chicago Review Press, 2014.

## Websites

To learn more about Presidential Perspectives, visit **booklinks.abdopublishing.com**. These links are routinely monitored and updated to provide the most current information available.

Visit **mycorelibrary.com** for free additional tools for teachers and students.

# INDEX

armed neutrality, 19–20
armistice, 31, 33, 36

Battle of Belleau Wood, 28
blockade, 11, 17

cabinet, 12, 25
Congress, 5, 7, 12–13, 16, 19–20, 21, 23, 24, 28, 32, 37–38
Council of National Defense, 25

daylight saving time, 26
declaration of war, 7, 11, 13, 15, 20, 23, 24

Ferdinand, Franz, 15, 20

Hitler, Adolf, 40
home front, 25–27

J. P. Morgan & Co., 17

League of Nations, 29, 33–35, 37, 39–40, 41
Liberty Loan, 26–27
Lodge, Henry Cabot, 35, 38
Lusitania, 7, 9, 11, 19, 20

Marshall, Thomas, 18
Mexican–American War, 11

neutrality, 7, 11, 16, 18, 20

pacifist, 27
Paris Peace Conference, 33–36

Selective Service Act, 24
socialist, 27
Sussex, 10

Treaty of Versailles, 36, 39–40
Tumulty, Joseph, 6–7

U-boat, 7–9, 13, 19, 20, 32
unrestricted submarine warfare, 19, 20

Wilson's 14 Points, 28, 29, 31, 36

Zimmermann, Arthur, 11

# ABOUT THE AUTHOR

Amanda Lanser is a freelance writer who lives in Minneapolis, Minnesota. She finds World War I fascinating. She is the author of books on a variety of topics from Pope Francis and climate change to boa constrictors and Ötzi the Iceman.